Little Inventions

THE TOILET

RAPHAËL FEJTÖ

FIREFLY BOOKS

A long time ago, most houses didn't have toilets like we do today. In Roman times, for example, people went to the bathroom together, in public toilets.

Then, the waste passed into tunnels filled with water that traveled underground to the river. This was done so the city didn't smell bad.

In European cities during the middle ages, canal systems were forgotten. People used chamber pots, and when they were full they threw them in the cellar... or right out onto the street!

In the country, there were outhouses out in the yard.

There were also toilets at the top of castle towers, but sometimes there was just a hole in the floor...

... so everything just fell along the
wall of the castle!

One day, in 1592, the queen of England, Elizabeth the 1st, found that it smelled so bad in her castle that she hired her godson, the writer John Harington, to do something about it.

He thought about the problem for a long time and had the idea to install a tank of water on the roof of her house, with a long pipe leading right to the toilet.

When the tap was opened, clean water flowed into the toilets, and dirty water was flushed out into a pit outside the house. It was a simple, yet very effective system!

Queen Elizabeth was thrilled,
because she didn't have to deal
with any horrible smells.

She urged her most important advisor to try this new invention.

But this didn't impress him, because he didn't really see the need: the bad smells didn't bother him at all!

In reality, aside from the queen, nobody appreciated this invention. Later, in France, King Louis the 14th preferred the *commode*, a wooden chair with a hole, and a pot underneath.

very comfortable velvet cushion

When he was hosting friends, he sat on his commode and could do his business, while discussing the business of the kingdom.

In 1775, Alexander Cummings, a Scotsman, submitted a patent for a toilet made of bent pipes, but it wasn't very successful, because it required a lot of water.

At the time, there still wasn't running water in houses. When you lived in the city, you had to go get water from the closest fountain or well.

Or you could pay water carriers to carry buckets but it was very expensive (which meant no one wanted to waste water in order to wash away their waste).

In Paris, water was sometimes taken directly from the river, but because people did their business in it, it was very polluted.

Paris became more and more dirty, and clean water became more and more expensive, so the Baron Haussmann,

20

an important planner, decided to create a modern sewer system; he had tunnels dug under the streets.

He also had big pipes installed that went from almost every house in the city, which dumped dirty water into the river outside of Paris.

The baron also brought clean water into houses ... Running water was finally installed.

As soon as access to water was no longer a problem, everyone started having toilets, and the flush toilet was perfected very quickly.

Reservoirs were installed above the basin with a chain attached that had to be pulled for water to run down to flush the dirty water away.

The reservoir is filled with water, and a plug prevents the water from flowing into the pipe connected to the basin.

removal →
toward the sewers

Then, when the chain is pulled, the plug lifts up, and the reservoir's water flows rapidly into the basin and pushes the waste out into the sewers.

Year after year, the flushing mechanism was perfected, and no one has to pull a chain anymore. There are many ways to flush!

lever system

double flush to conserve water

infrared system

I SAID **FLUSH!**

voice activated

And you?
What's your favorite kind of

TOILET

?

There you go! Now you know everything about the invention of the toilet!

So, do you remember everything you read?

Play the MEMORY game
to see what you remember!

MEMORY GAME

1. Where did the Ancient Romans do their private business?

2. During the Middle Ages, where did people empty their chamber pots?

3. Who developed the first flush toilet?

4. What was the name of the chair in which Louis the 14th did his business?

5. When did the flush toilet really take off?

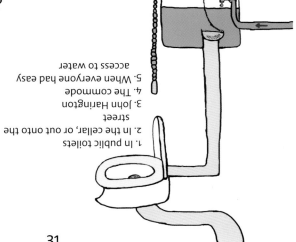

1. In public toilets
2. In the cellar, or out onto the street
3. John Harington
4. The commode
5. When everyone had easy access to water

A FIREFLY BOOK

Published by Firefly Books Ltd. 2016

Source edition © 2015 La Chausse d'eau, ÉDITIONS PLAY BAC, 33 rue du Petit-Musc, 75004, Paris, France, 2015

This translated edition copyright © 2016 Firefly Books

First printing

Publisher Cataloging-in-Publication Data (U.S.)

Names: Fejtö, Raphaël, author. | Greenspoon, Golda, translator. | Mersereau, Claudine, translator.
Title: Toilet / Raphaël Fejtö.
Description: Richmond Hill, Ontario, Canada : Firefly Books, 2016. | Series: Little Inventions | Originally published by Éditions Play Bac, Paris, 2015 as Les p'tites inventions: Chasse D'eau | Summary: "This brief history on one of the small, overlooked inventions we use in our everyday lives, in a six-part series is geared toward children. With fun and quirky illustrations and dialog, it also comes with a memory quiz to ensure children retain what they learn" -- Provided by publisher.
Identifiers: ISBN 978-1-77085-750-6 (hardcover)
Subjects: LCSH: Toilets – History -- Juvenile literature.
Classification: LCC TH6498.F458 |DDC 644.6 – dc23

Library and Archives Canada Cataloguing in Publication

Fejtö, Raphaël
[Chasse d'eau. English]
     The toilet / Raphaël Fejtö.
(Little inventions)
Translation of: La chasse d'eau.
ISBN 978-1-77085-750-6 (bound)
     1. Toilets--History--Juvenile literature. I. Title.
II. Title: Chasse d'eau. English.
TH6498.F4613 2016   j696'.182   C2016-900071-0

Published in the United States by
Firefly Books (U.S.) Inc.
P.O. Box 1338, Ellicott Station
Buffalo, New York 14205

Published in Canada by
Firefly Books Ltd.
50 Staples Avenue, Unit 1
Richmond Hill, Ontario L4B 0A7

Printed in China

playBac

les p'tites inventions